THE
MENTORING
ADVANTAGE

THE MENTORING ADVANTAGE

How to Help Your Career Soar to New Heights

Pam Grout

SkillPath Publications
Mission, KS

Project Editor: Kelly Scanlon

Editor: Jane Doyle Guthrie

Cover and Book Design: Rod Hankins

Cover Illustration: Steve Shamburger

ISBN: 1-878542-99-0

10 9 8 7 6 5 4 3 2   06 07 08 09 10

Printed in the United States of America

We are each of us angels with only one wing.
And we can only fly embracing each other.

—*Luciano De Crescenzo*

There are companions and helpers along the way. One pilgrim may help another as when a blind man carries one who is lame upon his back, so that together they may make a pilgrimage that neither could have made alone.

—*Sheldon B. Kopp*

Contents

Introduction

The poet John Donne was right: Not only is "no man an island," but no man, or woman, can hope to create a successful life without connecting with many different people. Examine the lives of many of the great masters and you'll find a long supporting cast who inspired them, prodded them, encouraged them, and perhaps even angered them enough to rise and make a difference.

Think about it—why are televised awards ceremonies getting so long these days? Because every Tom Hanks, Dick Burton, and Deborah Harry who wins something has to thank everyone who helped. Look at the dedication page of most books. Even though writing can be one of the most solitary of activities, there's always a list of somebodies—a loving spouse, an inspiring teacher, a supportive editor—without whom the project would never have blossomed.

Through our beneficial, nurturing relationships with others, we learn to successfully earn a living, build a family, cope with problems, and enjoy life. We all stand on the shoulders of others at various times while we're learning and growing and developing new roles for ourselves.

That's what mentoring is about. Finding people to help you live your dreams. Mentors—thanks to who or what they know—have the power to give your goals both roots and wings. Mentors can teach skills, open doors, cut red tape, provide exposure, and serve as much-needed cheerleaders and sounding boards.

According to Dr. Linda Phillips-Jones, a career development consultant in California, finding and making use of the right mentor is the most critical step a person can take in his or her career. It's certainly a strategy that's been around for centuries—although the word "mentor" wasn't always used. In fact, the word first appeared in Greek mythology. Mentor, a friend and advisor to Odysseus, took on the task of guarding and teaching the great man's son, Telemachus.

Some famous mentoring relationships turned out pretty well, you'll agree. Michelangelo, for example, apprenticed himself to Leonardo da Vinci, who years before had been apprenticed to artist and teacher Andrea del Verrocchio. Sigmund Freud kept a picture of his mentor, Dr. Jean Charcot, on the wall of his study. According to Freud, it was

Charcot who taught him to trust in his own research, even when it went against the prevailing beliefs of his time. Freud once wrote that Charcot helped him to "look at the same things again and again until they themselves began to speak." And, of course, Freud went on to mentor Carl Jung and other pioneers in the study of the mind.

The mentoring system provides a wonderful opportunity to trust those ahead of us on the path we want to take, using their knowledge to build upon and draw us along. By absorbing their wisdom, we eventually can add our own unique contribution to the chain. In this book, you'll not only learn strategies for finding a mentor, but tips for cementing that all-important relationship and for carrying on the flame.

Chapter 1

Tapping the
Mentor
Advantage

entors can provide wisdom, inspiration, and even a push in the right direction. Besides that, a mentor who believes you have great potential can inspire you to believe in yourself and to try harder at things. This special relationship offers many advantages:

- **Mentors provide powerful role models.** A role model presents irrefutable evidence that success is possible. Many people have begun their climb up the career ladder by first recognizing that if somebody else could do it, they can too.

- **Mentors provide a safe nest.** While still a fledgling, you need someone looking out for you, someone who realizes that your wings are just developing. The mentoring system supplies that all-important nurturing while you are learning to fly.

- **Mentors provide support.** Nothing is more powerful than knowing somebody out there believes in you. Besides the "feel good" part, there's also a very practical side to a mentor's advocacy: A supportive teacher or boss can loosen many sorts of career bottlenecks.

  Jean, for example, was hand-picked by her well-respected geometry professor as a teaching assistant. Ironically, she recently had considered getting out of math because she was starting to doubt herself and her abilities and wondered whether there was a place for her in the field. This professor reconfirmed her original belief and bolstered her career.

- **Mentors provide a heritage and tradition of skills.** Look at the history books and you'll see countless examples of masters passing on their crafts to eager apprentices. Today the system works a little differently, but no matter what you want to master— designing with your new graphics software or becoming a travel writer—there are mentors waiting to show you the inside track.

  John Wooden, former basketball coach for UCLA, credits his mentor, Ward "Piggy" Lambert of Purdue, with teaching him everything he used to become a celebrated college coach.

- **Mentors provide opportunities and resources.** When Margaret Mead was a student at Columbia University, she chose one of her anthropology professors as a mentor. Among other benefits, he secured a ticket for her to the South Pacific, where she launched her illustrious career. Mentors—thanks to their connections—can often steer you into the places you need to go.

- **Mentors provide a map.** We all look to others for guidance on how to live. The mapping starts in infancy, with direct imitation of our parents, siblings, and other early childhood influences. In mentoring, we consciously revive this process. If you want to learn or change your behavior, you observe someone who is "there" and attempt to distill the essence.

When Anthony Robbins, bestselling author of *Unlimited Power* and other books, decided he wanted to lose weight, for example, he zeroed in on people who not only had taken off pounds but also had kept them off for many years. He asked them everything he could think of to discover the secrets of their success. Once he spelled it out, he could adopt those practices for himself.

Robbins calls this process "modeling," but it's also a significant part of mentoring: building on the strengths that others have already demonstrated. Robbins believes you can learn anything very quickly by modeling the successes of others (even to the point of walking on a bed of hot coals, which he learned how to do from masters in Polynesia!).

As you can see, working with a mentor (or mentors) can expand your possibilities tremendously. As you've probably also picked up on, you have an important part to play as a protégé—to keep your eyes open for opportunities, and to commit yourself energetically to the process.

When Steven Spielberg was a kid of 17, he took a tour of Universal Studios. He sneaked off to watch the filming of a real movie and ended up meeting the head of the editorial department, who talked with him for an hour.

The next day young Steven donned a suit, brought along his father's briefcase (containing a sandwich and two candy bars), and returned to the lot as if he belonged there. He found an abandoned trailer and, using some plastic letters, put "Steven Spielberg, Director" on the door. He went on to spend the summer meeting directors, writers, and editors, lingering at the edges of the world he craved. He learned from every conversation and observed firsthand what worked and what didn't in moviemaking.

Napoleon Hill, bestselling author of *Think and Grow Rich*, says he never entirely divested himself of his habit of hero worship, believing the next best thing to being great is to emulate the great. In his words, he reshaped his character by imitating the nine men whose lives and life-works were most impressive to him.

Every night, before nodding off to sleep, he held an imaginary council meeting with Ralph Waldo Emerson, Thomas Paine, Thomas Edison, Charles Darwin, Abraham Lincoln, Luther Burbank, Napoleon Bonaparte, Henry Ford, and Andrew Carnegie. From Edison, he wanted to acquire a spirit of faith; from Lincoln, a keen sense of justice, untiring patience, a sense of humor, and so forth. Although these council meetings were completely imaginary, they had a profound effect on Hill's life.

The point is that mentoring can take many forms, and by focusing on its advantages, you can help yourself commit to the work involved. You'll be developing observational and analytic skills that will put a new source of strength at your fingertips. When you're sorting out a new situation or when a tough decision comes up, you can put yourself in your mentor's shoes. You can ask yourself, what would my mentor do? Don't worry about whether your conclusions are what he or she may really do—it's what *you* would do being the kind of person you want to be.

With a glimpse now of how mentoring changes lives, it's time to look more closely at where it all begins—with you, the prospective protégé.

Exercise #1

Targeting Your Role Models

1. Think about all the people you know from every
   area of your life. Which ones would you consider to
   be role models? Why?

   _____

   _____

   _____

   _____

   _____

   _____

   _____

2. If you could ask each of these people a question,
   what would it be? Why?

   _____

   _____

   _____

   _____

   _____

   _____

   _____

3. In what ways could these people support you? Could they open doors or teach you a skill?

_____

_____

_____

_____

_____

_____

_____

_____

Chapter 2

Developing
Yourself
As a Protégé

The mentoring system works a little like building blocks. The bottom blocks provide support for the top blocks, but both tiers play a significant role in holding up the staircase or bridge or skyscraper to which they belong. Each piece of the building block tower is a vital part of the whole. Each piece—mentor and protégé—is essential to building and sustaining the mentoring relationship. Before you go shopping for this special tutor or coach, therefore, it's a good idea to take a look at yourself as protégé material.

The exercise on the next page will help you get started with this self-analysis.

Exercise #2

Am I Protégé Material?

Read through the following list of statements and see whether you agree or disagree with each one. Be honest!

Agree   Disagree

☐   ☐   1. My mentoring goals are clearly defined.

☐   ☐   2. I'm willing to take directions.

☐   ☐   3. I'm good at accepting help.

☐   ☐   4. I truly hear what other people say.

☐   ☐   5. I know how to follow directions.

☐   ☐   6. I'm grateful, quick to say "thanks."

☐   ☐   7. I'm willing to speak up when necessary.

☐   ☐   8. I'm willing to ask for help.

☐   ☐   9. I believe in myself and have a lot to offer a mentor.

☐   ☐   10. I follow through with assignments.

☐   ☐   11. I'm a good team player.

☐   ☐   12. I'm willing to share credit for jobs well done.

Your answers to the previous exercise are important, because these statements lay out the basic ingredients for a promising protégé candidate. When you examine your responses to these "ground rules," you may see, for example, that you're basically good protégé material, but your team skills might benefit from a little sprucing up. Take time to think through your answers and ask whether you're really willing to make the commitment that becoming a protégé requires. Be open to the insights that self-examination offers you. Are you resistant to accepting help from others? Why? Is there some way to strike a balance between dependence and independence?

Once you've sized up your prospects as a protégé, the next step is determining what you'd want out of such a partnership. What a person wants and needs in a mentoring relationship can be unclear sometimes, and the assumptions about the relationship can be inconsistent. It's important, therefore, to assess yourself in this way too. Here are some questions you must ask yourself:

1. **At what rung of the career ladder are you now?** Are you just starting out? Are you returning to the workforce for a second time? Or are you looking for ways to move up in your present organization?

2. **Are there any foreseeable turning points in your career?** Mentors can be especially important at crisis periods or turning points—making a career change, choosing a specialty, sitting on the verge of a promotion, and so on.

3. **What exactly are your career goals?** Tap into your dreams here—have you set your sights on upper management? Is your own business the pot of gold you're striving for? Do you want to develop a very specialized kind of expertise?

4. **What are your strengths and weaknesses?** Which areas need fine-tuning? Not only will these answers help you determine what type of mentor to seek out, but they will help define the benefits you can offer to potential mentors.

5. **How have you dealt with intimate relationships in the past?** A mentoring relationship can be an intimate one, sometimes as potent as those you carry on with family and close friends. Examine your patterns in initiating, maintaining, and ending relationships. Is the quality satisfactory? Or maybe you need mentoring in learning to be intimate?

6. **Which of your current relationships might be developed into a mentoring relationship?** Within your immediate network lies a host of talent. You don't have to stop there, but it's important to pan the gold in your own stream first.

7. **What type of relationship would best serve you?** That is, would you like a coach—someone to counsel you on your current assignments, or someone to give you feedback and appraise your progress? Or perhaps a financial sponsor would better serve your purpose—someone who can back you while believing in your talents. Some protégés would rather have a peer, a successful colleague on the same level who can offer empathy as well as support. (Keep in mind that you don't have to choose just one; at different points in your career, different kinds of mentors may serve you best.)

8. **Are you willing to pay your dues?** A mentor will probably want something in return. Remember that mentoring is reciprocal.

Exercise #3 gives you an opportunity to write your own responses to these questions.

Exercise#3

What Do I Want and Need in a Mentoring Relationship?

Carefully consider each of the following questions and write honest and realistic responses.

1. Where am I on the career ladder? _____

_____

_____

_____

_____

_____

2. Do I foresee a career change in my future? _____

_____

_____

_____

_____

3. What are my career goals? _____

_____

_____

_____

_____

4. What are my strengths? _____

_____

_____

_____

_____

5. How do I deal with intimate relationships? _____

_____

_____

_____

_____

6. Could any of my current relationships develop into a mentoring relationship? _____

_____

_____

_____

_____

_____

_____

_____

7. What type of mentoring relationship would be best for me? _____

_____

_____

_____

_____

_____

_____

_____

8. Will I be able to reciprocate? _____

_____

_____

_____

_____

_____

Now that you've challenged yourself to seek out the protégé waiting within, it's time to consider how to seek out a mentor to round out the team.

Chapter 3

Selecting the
Right
Mentor for You

Some wishful protégés make the mistake of believing a mentor must find them. They sit back like wallflowers, passively waiting to be approached and chosen like a piece of fine china.

While it's true that mentors can and sometimes do initiate relationships with potential protégés, there are many specific ways you can make yourself competitive in the "mentor market." Finding a mentor on your own timeline requires action as well as vision, planning, and sensitivity.

When she was a student at Columbia University, Margaret Mead was drawn to anthropologist Franz Boas. Through him, she realized, she could become part of a handful of scholars in a field just starting to gain acceptance and prestige in America. In her autobiography, *Blackberry Winter,* Mead notes that her strategy was to nod thoughtfully every time Boas made a point in class. It worked. He was impressed, and went out of his way to give her special attention.

As you are considering your options, it's also important to know and reflect on the cardinal rules of mentoring:

1. **No man or woman can be everything.** Mentoring is not about snagging your personal superhero; it's about building relationships that are mutually satisfying and beneficial to both partners. If necessary, pick out several people for several different traits: communicating clearly, delegating responsibility effectively, or talking to groups without embarrassment.

2. **Pedestals are dangerous and easy to fall from.** Remember the whole point of having a mentor is to improve yourself—to better *become* yourself. The last thing you want is to be a copy of someone else. No one is perfect, and if you put someone else on a pedestal, you can only fail in comparison.

3. Having a mentor takes work on the protégé's part.
Some people mistakenly think that having a mentor is
the easy way to get ahead, though it actually involves
time and extra work. It means stretching your limits,
taking on new commitments and risks. Mentors are often
demanding.

In considering this, it's important to examine your
reasons for wanting a mentor. Are you trying to avoid
learning something for yourself? Are you trying to shirk
responsibility for something you need to do?

4. Mentoring is a two-way street. Mentors and protégés
each get much out of the relationship. Because both of
you are active partners (protégés aren't just on the
receiving end), it's a mutually satisfying, mutually
beneficial setup.

5. Protégés aren't just trying to become clones. Mentors
with skill or authority deserve to be listened to, but each
member of the partnership retains unique interests and
views. Modeling yourself after someone admirable and
successful is certainly one of the aspects of interacting
with a mentor, but remember that the goal here is
growth—not imitation.

Now that you're armed with resolve and insight, where do
you look for a mentor? Mentors and protégés meet
everywhere. Although the most common ground is work,
many of these duos connect through community activities
and special interest groups, or even on the tennis courts.
Usually the relationships evolve through shared interests,
admiration, or job demands.

Once you've zeroed in on what you'd like to develop and where you'd like to grow, the next stage is finding someone who has already mastered the skills or traits you aspire toward. For example, if your life seems too chaotic, look for someone who is well-organized and always gets things taken care of.

With your growth area in mind, make a list of people who fit the qualifications, but don't worry about making contacts with them yet. At this point, it's just important to write down a few names, because once you can put a name and a face on the qualities or abilities you're drawn to, you'll begin to realize that this could be you too. Use Exercise #4 to start your name gathering.

Possible Mentor Candidates

1. People who have the trait I want to develop:

  A. _____

  B. _____

  C. _____

2. People who've already mastered the skill I need:

  A. _____

  B. _____

  C. _____

3. People who possess the personality attributes I admire:

  A. _____

  B. _____

  C. _____

4. People who embrace areas of life that I've neglected and left underdeveloped:

  A. _____

  B. _____

  C. _____

With your prospects fine-tuned through this listing exercise (you may have seen the same name reappearing on each list), it's time to do your homework. Learn your prospective mentor's story. You can find this out through casual conversation, by talking to his or her acquaintances, and if he or she is well known, through books and newspapers at the library.

One enterprising protégé went so far as to find the college yearbook of his first choice as a mentor. He discovered that the mentor candidate had been in the band, so the protégé invited the would-be mentor to play in his small ensemble. This brought the protégé to close terms with the mentor through a different avenue than business. As fellow musicians, they were free of the barriers and hierarchies of the workplace.

Once you know your potential mentor's background, it's important to ask yourself the following questions before approaching him or her:

- Who do you know that your mentor knows?
- What qualities do you already have that your mentor has?
- How can you become more visible to your mentor?
- Does your mentor appreciate creative approaches?
- Where does your mentor go when not working?
- What other interests does your mentor have?
- What kind of protégés has your mentor taken on in the past?
- What could you offer to enhance your mentor's life?

Though you may not find all the answers, this is the sort of information that will put you on the playing field. To access the advantages of mentorship, you should give yourself some advantages in the line-up.

The next step is to actually take the plunge, to approach the person you've chosen as a potential mentor. Here are some tips:

- If the person is "all business" and doesn't "do lunch," you're just about going to have to write a letter or make your approach in a business situation (e.g., make an appointment, make the connection at a meeting, etc.)

- If you know the person belongs to clubs or a gym or walks in the park, consider including these places in your routine to increase your chances of striking up a conversation. Follow this advice only if it seems appropriate for your situation.

- Who do you know in common? Perhaps that person would be willing to make the introduction.

When you do make the approach, here are some guidelines to keep in mind:

- **Be honest.** Tell a potential mentor that your respect his or her work and would like to get to know him or her better.

- **Be specific.** Don't just say, "Hey, I really think you're great." Say something like, "I really like the way you handled the Stevens account." That way the potential mentor knows that you've taken the time to find out something related to his or her work.

- **Offer to help.** Once you know your potential mentor's story, you probably have a good idea what things he or she might need help with. For example, if a prospective mentor is writing a book, offer to do some research. It's hard for anyone to refuse free help.

Watch out for certain no-nos when approaching your mentor:

1. **"Hi, I'm Lily Nelson, your next protégé."** As tempting as it might be to call up the president of your company and ask point blank if she'd like to be your mentor, realize that a mentoring relationship isn't always called by its given name. The words "mentor" and "protégé" are loaded. Sometimes people who might otherwise agree to help you don't feel comfortable being called a "mentor."

2. **"You think I should brush up my résumé? No way—I just had it done by a professional service."** One of the worst mistakes a protégé can make is to seek advice and then fail to follow it. Even if you don't follow the mentor's counsel, let him or her know it was helpful.

3. **"If you won't be my mentor, I might get fired and end up on the streets."** Don't be too obvious or too desperate. Needy protégés are intimidating and a little off-putting.

4. **"I have so much to offer. My father was a bigwig with the police department. And my mom was a Sunday school teacher. And then there's my uncle who ... Say, did I tell you about my grandfather?"** Don't oversell yourself with excessive talking or a canned sales pitch. Be willing to listen and adapt your request to what your mentor has to offer.

5. **"Yes, you'll work with me? Well, let me just get through with my final and then I've got this big report to finish up. What's your dayplanner like next Labor Day?"** Once a prospective mentor shows interest in you, don't wait to jump on the bandwagon. Move toward a commitment before he or she loses interest or doubts your earnestness.

6. "Mr. Anderson's too busy to talk to me? Okay, I promise never to call him ever again." Don't give up easily. Maybe your first letter didn't get through, but at least your name now rings a bell. Stick with it—everybody admires a little chutzpah.

With timing and insight, you can forge a link with just the right mentor for a short- or long-term partnership, whichever you need at the moment. If you then put your shoulder into making the relationship work, you're not only investing in personal growth but also probably tapping into a larger pool of future prospective mentors.

Chapter 4

Making the
Mentoring
Relationship Work

I t goes without saying that some relationships work better than others. In the past, you may have tended to accept the quality of certain relationships as "the way it is," as an immovable inevitability. Your mentoring relationship, however, deserves your full concern and attention—because the payoff can be so great, the loss can too if things deteriorate or just don't move forward.

You can do several things to improve the quality of your relationship with your mentor:

1. **Develop a rapport.** Don't rush right in and pick your mentor's brain. A mentoring relationship, like any close association, takes time to blossom. You must develop trust, demonstrate your commitment, and prove yourself a capable protégé. Be willing to spend the time it takes.

2. **Be observant.** Everything doesn't have to be spelled out in red ink. Instead of swamping your mentor with questions, watch how he or she handles significant situations. Sure, you can ask point blank, "How do you deal with difficult customers?" But there's also an advantage to observing your mentor in action. By paying close attention, you may gain insights that he or she may not possess. As a result of habit and experience, your mentor may not be consciously aware of how he or she deals with various situations. Your observations and input might prove helpful and even encourage your mentor to take you along to other events.

3. **Make yourself invaluable.** By communicating what you like and what you observe as the two of you work together, your mentor can improve at the same time he or she is helping you to do so. Be careful not to criticize, but to share thoughtful observations about the way things are accomplished. Offer to pitch in when appropriate, and be willing to work free and late. Make sure that this stays a mutually agreeable and profitable relationship.

4. **Follow the rules of any good relationship.** Be predictable. Be clear. Take promises seriously. Be honest. Let's hear it for the golden rule!

5. **Plan interesting adventures together.** If your mentor loves to read science fiction, check out the latest bestseller and be willing to discuss it. If your mentor is a skydiver, maybe it's time to get out a parachute. Remember, this partnership is about stretching your horizons, and both mentors and protégés can offer stimulating new activities to the team.

6. **Eschew competition.** Mentoring is not about axing others up to get ahead. It's about working with someone special for mutual gratification, satisfaction, and growth.

Exercise #5

Creating a Vision

An effective bonding exercise is to create a vision for your mentoring relationship. There is power in two, and you might as well utilize it.

1. First, adopt a motto such as "Together, we can solve miracles."

   Write your motto here: _____

   _____

   _____

   _____

   _____

   _____

   _____

2. Now, working separately, write a series of short sentences that describe what you'd like to accomplish in the mentoring relationship. These will become your mission statements. Include qualities you already have and those you wish you had. Write each sentence in the present tense, as if it were already happening. Cast each as a positive statement, writing "We settle our differences peacefully" rather than "We don't fight."

Here are some other examples:

- "Together, we improve our company's bottom line."
- "We find better benefits for all employees."
- "We develop a speakers series from within the company."

Write your goals for the relationship here. (Don't forget to have your mentor compile a list as well.)

_____

_____

_____

_____

_____

_____

_____

_____

_____

_____

3. When both of you have finished, share your sentences. Note the items you have in common and underline them. When you realize the many ways in which this relationship is important, the work you do will double exponentially.

4. On your own, as a step toward feeling closer to your mentor, make a list of the positive qualities he or she has. Why do you admire this person? How did he or she develop these qualities? Next, make a list of your own qualities. Often, you'll discover similarities with your mentor—people tend to admire those whose interests and qualities relate to their own. Finally, ask yourself what it is that you like about one or more of these qualities. Why would they help you in what you want to do?

My Mentor's Positive Qualities

_____

_____

_____

_____

_____

_____

_____

My Positive Qualities

_____

_____

_____

_____

_____

_____

_____

5. Another helpful step in ensuring a healthy, growth-oriented partnership is to examine your expectations and perhaps reveal some potential stumbling blocks. For example, identify each of these statements as "true" or "false":

T F

☐ ☐ 1. Avoiding disagreements is a good goal for our mentoring relationship.

☐ ☐ 2. Mentoring relationships need to be close and last forever.

☐ ☐ 3. Getting approval means we have a good relationship.

☐ ☐ 4. Mentors should be older than their protégés.

☐ ☐ 5. A good mentoring relationship is one in which we agree easily.

☐ ☐ 6. Mentors should be in the same field as their protégés.

☐ ☐ 7. Mentors have to be perfect.

☐ ☐ 8. Mentors have to be business successes.

Did you mentally check off any of these as "true"? Every one of them is false. And here's why:

1. It's counterproductive to sweep problems under the rug. In fact, it's when learning to deal with problems that we gain the most insight about our mentors and ourselves.

2. Mentoring relationships do *not* need to be particularly close, and their length can vary. Sigmund Freud, for example, worked with his mentor for less than five months.

3. All mentoring relationships will encounter some disagreement and disappointment. The key is in learning how to handle it.

4. Mentors are often older than their protégés, but they certainly can be the same age or even younger. What's important is that the mentor has skills, knowledge, or power that the protégé needs.

5. Expecting or valuing effortless agreement is like judging a good road as the one that's easy to build. A good relationship has nothing to do with ease.

6. Perhaps you're a cookie baker and your mentor is a mosaic artist, but you admire him because he believes in doing things differently—all of his mosaics are wildly creative and you want your cookies to be wildly creative. No problem.

7. You're not looking for someone to copy—just someone to learn from, someone to model yourself after. Always remember that you're trying to build on what this person has already established. Edison had to work successfully with electricity before somebody could invent a CD player.

8. What you value and admire in your mentors, and where you have the potential to grow the most with them, can be unrelated to business. It may eventually tie in or translate to a professional advantage, but don't be short-sighted in this regard when you decide whether or not to pursue a mentoring opportunity.

By now you know that a mentoring relationship isn't perfect and isn't meant to be. Gail Sheehy said it well in *Passages:* "Just as a child must inevitably see a parent as less than the repository of all the world's wisdom, so must the apprentice eventually repudiate the mentor in order to believe in her independence." In the meantime, though, here are some exercises for aiding communication and heading off problems before they crop up:

- **Focus on an emotional state you would like your mentor to feel and adopt it for yourself.** For example, your mentor is more likely to show concern for you if you show concern for him or her; likewise, your mentor is more apt to be optimistic if you show optimism.

- **Recall a time, place, and circumstance when your morale was high.** Start behaving now as if you were back in that situation. If you're a weekend tennis warrior, for example, mentally place yourself on the tennis court where you feel confident and in command. This can keep you charged up and focused as a protégé.

- **Make listening contracts.** Agree that each person is allowed a certain period of time to talk. Even without ground rules, self-restraint helps. When you've set up a forum in advance, it helps to avoid verbal logjams. You can facilitate clear communication with your mentor by setting up a regular time, place, and process for getting issues on the table.

- **Try to imagine the other person's situation and assume his or her role.** It helps to be as explicit as possible when you're doing this. With practice, you can more easily understand contrary points of view.

After successfully participating as a protégé in one or more mentoring relationships, you may feel the stirrings to take on a new challenge—to be a mentor yourself. Doing so is a priceless way to say "thank you" to those who've invested in you as mentors, and it's the only way the system perpetuates.

Chapter 5

Becoming a
Mentor
Yourself

The last step in the mentoring process is to become one yourself. Whether you realize it or not, you are probably informally mentoring several people right now—your children, your secretary, the members of a committee you're in charge of.

Your next challenge may be to consciously take someone under your wing, but why?

- A protégé can help you finish your life's work.
- There's great satisfaction in helping others.
- Your company (or organization, or neighborhood) will benefit.
- By taking on a protégé, you can repay your own debts to a mentor.

It's also wise to examine yourself as a prospective mentor just as you did as a prospective protégé. For example, ask yourself:

1. Do I have an ulterior motive for wanting to relate to this person?
2. Is my interest conditional?
3. Am I trying to escape something that I don't want to do myself?
4. Am I hoping to change this person?
5. Do I need this person to help me make up for a deficiency in myself?

If you answered "yes" to any of these questions, you may need to rethink whether you're ready to become a mentor at this time.

If, however, you decide to take the plunge, here are some tips to ensure success:

- **Actions speak louder than words.** You can talk all you want about doing something a certain way, but it's better to demonstrate with actions. Bill Marriott wants the employees of the Marriott Corporation to care about customers; therefore, he travels more than 200,000 miles a year visiting his hotels *showing* employees how to take care of customers. He lives his vision.

  Ray Kroc, founder of McDonald's, also instilled his vision through example. Once, on his way back to the office from an important lunch, Kroc asked his driver to pass through several McDonald's parking lots. In one, he spotted paper caught up in some shrubs along the outer fence. He went to the nearest pay phone, got the name of the manager, and called him to offer help in picking up the trash. Ray Kroc in his expensive business suit and the young manager in his uniform met in the parking lot, got on their hands and knees, and collected the windblown trash.

- **Liberate people to do what is required of them.** This is the most effective and humane way of motivating your protégés. A good mentor is the "servant" of his or her students by removing obstacles that prevent them from doing their jobs.

- **Believe in yourself enough to encourage contrary opinions.** Part of being a mentor is serving as a sounding board and as "home port" to someone trying to sort through his or her options.

- **Provide and maintain momentum.** Whether you're aware of it or not, your actions and energy are always influencing other people—particularly protégés who look up to you. You can set the pace of an entire committee by being aware of your own energy and words.

- **Don't look for clones of yourself.** Allow others to express their own gifts. Induce freedom, not paralysis.

- **Commit to the sacred nature of the relationship.** Be open to a variety of personalities and unusual ideas. Tolerate risk and forgive errors.

- **Give constant care to the growth and progress of each protégé.** Allow them to be their own persons and help them attain their personal goals.

- **Keep the lines of communication open.** Maximize the good, minimize the bad.

- **Don't expect anyone to be perfect.** We're only human, and a spirit of tolerance for differences and imperfections makes relationships stronger, work easier to get done.

- **Offer unlimited support and strength on which protégés can draw.** Don't forget to provide compliments. Even when mistakes are made, look for the good. There is always something that can be praised. Make it clear that you support your protégé.

- **Provide lots of public affirmation.** People need to hear that they're doing a good job. They also need to be reassured around other people.

- **Expect to invest a great deal of time and energy in your relationships.** Good mentoring relationships don't just happen. They are created.

Exercise #6

Preparing to Become a Mentor

1. List any special knowledge or skills that you could share with others.

_____

_____

_____

_____

_____

_____

2. Do you know anyone who could benefit from your knowledge or skills. List those peope here.

_____

_____

_____

_____

_____

_____

3. From your responses to the two previous questions, choose the mentoring situation that you'd most like to pursue. Then write a plan for initiating the relationship.

_____

_____

_____

_____

_____

_____

_____

_____

_____

4. Plot out some ways you could convey the knowledge or skills you have to share.

_____

_____

_____

_____

_____

_____

_____

_____

Bibliography

Belasco, James A. *Teaching the Elephant to Dance: Empowering Change in Your Organization*. New York: Crown Publishers, 1990.

Brooks, Michael. *The Power of Business Rapport: Using NLP Technology to Make More Money, Sell Yourself and Your Product and Move Ahead in Business*. New York: HarperCollins, 1991.

Buscaglia, Leo. *Loving Each Other: The Challenge of Human Relationships*. Thorofare, NJ: Slack Inc., 1984.

De Pree, Max. *Leadership Is an Art*. New York: Doubleday, 1989.

Fisher, Roger, and Scott Brown. *Getting Together: Building a Relationship That Gets to Yes*. Boston: Houghton Mifflin, 1988.

Evans, Thomas W. *Mentors: Making a Difference in Our Public Schools*. Princeton, NJ: Peterson's Guides, 1992.

Hill, Napoleon. *Think and Grow Rich*. New York: Fawcett Crest, 1960.

Hollander, Edwin P. *Leadership Dynamics: A Practical Guide to Effective Relationships*. New York: Free Press, 1978.

Josselson, Ruthellen. *The Space Between Us: Exploring the Dimensions of Human Relationships*. San Francisco: Jossey-Bass, 1992.

Leefeldt, Christine, and Ernest Callenbach. *The Art of Friendship*. New York: Pantheon Books, 1979.

Mead, Margaret. *Blackberry Winter: My Earlier Years*. New York: Morrow, 1972.

Phillips-Jones, Linda. *Mentors and Protégés*. New York: Arbor House, 1982.

Robbins, Anthony. *Unlimited Power*. New York: Fawcett Columbine, 1987.

Sheehy, Gail. *Passages: Predictable Causes of Adult Life*. Toronto: Bantam, 1977.

Zey, Michael G. *Winning With People: Building Lifelong Professional and Personal Success Through the Supporting Cast Principle*. Los Angeles: J. P. Tarcher, 1990.

Available From SkillPath Publications

Self-Study Sourcebooks

Aim First: Get Focused and Fired Up to Follow Through on Your Goals *by Lee T. Silber*

The Business and Technical Writer's Guide *by Robert McGraw*

Climbing the Corporate Ladder: What You Need to Know and Do to Be a Promotable Person *by Barbara Pachter and Marjorie Brody*

Coping With Supervisory Nightmares: 12 Common Nightmares of Leadership and What You Can Do About Them *by Michael and Deborah Singer Dobson*

Defeating Procrastination: 52 Fail-Safe Tips for Keeping Time on Your Side *by Marlene Caroselli, Ed.D.*

Discovering Your Purpose *by Ivy Haley*

Going for the Gold: Winning the Gold Medal for Financial Independence *by Lesley D. Bissett, CFP*

Having Something to Say When You Have to Say Something: The Art of Organizing Your Presentation *by Randy Horn*

Info-Flood: How to Swim in a Sea of Information Without Going Under *by Marlene Caroselli, Ed.D.*

The Innovative Secretary *by Marlene Caroselli, Ed.D.*

Letters & Memos: Just Like That! *by Dave Davies*

Mastering the Art of Communication: Your Keys to Developing a More Effective Personal Style *by Michelle Fairfield Poley*

Organized for Success! 95 Tips for Taking Control of Your Time, Your Space, and Your Life *by Nanci McGraw*

A Passion to Lead! How to Develop Your Natural Leadership Ability *by Michael Plumstead*

P.E.R.S.U.A.D.E.: Communication Strategies That Move People to Action *by Marlene Caroselli, Ed.D.*

Productivity Power: 250 Great Ideas for Being More Productive *by Jim Temme*

Promoting Yourself: 50 Ways to Increase Your Prestige, Power, and Paycheck *by Marlene Caroselli, Ed.D.*

Proof Positive: How to Find Errors Before They Embarrass You *by Karen L. Anderson*

Risk-Taking: 50 Ways to Turn Risks Into Rewards *by Marlene Caroselli, Ed.D. and David Harris*

Speak Up and Stand Out: How to Make Effective Presentations *by Nanci McGraw*

Stress Control: How You Can Find Relief From Life's Daily Stress *by Steve Bell*

Total Quality Customer Service: How to Make It Your Way of Life *by Jim Temme*

Write It Right! A Guide for Clear and Correct Writing *by Richard Andersen and Helene Hinis*

Your Total Communication Image *by Janet Signe Olson, Ph.D.*

Handbooks

The ABC's of Empowered Teams: Building Blocks for Success *by Mark Towers*

Assert Yourself! Developing Power-Packed Communication Skills to Make Your Points Clearly, Confidently, and Persuasively *by Lisa Contini*

Breaking the Ice: How to Improve Your On-the-Spot Communication Skills
by Deborah Shouse

The Care and Keeping of Customers: A Treasury of Facts, Tips, and Proven Techniques for Keeping Your Customers Coming BACK! *by Roy Lantz*

Challenging Change: Five Steps for Dealing With Change *by Holly DeForest and Mary Steinberg*

Dynamic Delegation: A Manager's Guide for Active Empowerment *by Mark Towers*

Every Woman's Guide to Career Success *by Denise M. Dudley*

Exploring Personality Styles: A Guide for Better Understanding Yourself and Your Colleagues *by Michael Dobson*

Grammar? No Problem! *by Dave Davies*

Great Openings and Closings: 28 Ways to Launch and Land Your Presentations With Punch, Power, and Pizazz *by Mari Pat Varga*

Hiring and Firing: What Every Manager Needs to Know *by Marlene Caroselli, Ed.D. with Laura Wyeth, Ms.Ed.*

How to Be a More Effective Group Communicator: Finding Your Role and Boosting Your Confidence in Group Situations *by Deborah Shouse*

How to Deal With Difficult People *by Paul Friedman*

Learning to Laugh at Work: The Power of Humor in the Workplace *by Robert McGraw*

Making Your Mark: How to Develop a Personal Marketing Plan for Becoming More Visible and More Appreciated at Work *by Deborah Shouse*

Meetings That Work *by Marlene Caroselli, Ed.D.*

The Mentoring Advantage: How to Help Your Career Soar to New Heights *by Pam Grout*

Minding Your Business Manners: Etiquette Tips for Presenting Yourself Professionally in Every Business Situation *by Marjorie Brody and Barbara Pachter*

Misspeller's Guide *by Joel and Ruth Schroeder*

Motivation in the Workplace: How to Motivate Workers to Peak Performance and Productivity *by Barbara Fielder*

NameTags Plus: Games You Can Play When People Don't Know What to Say *by Deborah Shouse*

Networking: How to Creatively Tap Your People Resources *by Colleen Clarke*

New & Improved! 25 Ways to Be More Creative and More Effective *by Pam Grout*

Power Write! A Practical Guide to Words That Work *by Helene Hinis*

The Power of Positivity: Eighty ways to energize your life *by Joel and Ruth Schroeder*

Putting Anger to Work For You *by Ruth and Joel Schroeder*

Reinventing Your Self: 28 Strategies for Coping With Change *by Mark Towers*

Saying "No" to Negativity: How to Manage Negativity in Yourself, Your Boss, and Your Co-Workers *by Zoie Kaye*

The Supervisor's Guide: The Everyday Guide to Coordinating People and Tasks *by Jerry Brown and Denise Dudley, Ph.D.*

Taking Charge: A Personal Guide to Managing Projects and Priorities *by Michal E. Feder*

Treasure Hunt: 10 Stepping Stones to a New and More Confident You! *by Pam Grout*

A Winning Attitude: How to Develop Your Most Important Asset! *by Michelle Fairfield Poley*

For more information, call 1-800-873-7545.

Notes

Notes

Notes

Notes